Unconscious Memories

Volume II
Dream into the Music

Kristen Andersen

BALBOA.PRESS
A DIVISION OF HAY HOUSE

Balboa Press books may be ordered through booksellers or by contacting:

Balboa Press
A Division of Hay House
1663 Liberty Drive
Bloomington, IN 47403
www.balboapress.com
844-682-1282

Images by: Kristen Andersen

Print information available on the last page.

ISBN: 978-1-9822-6812-1 (sc)
ISBN: 978-1-9822-6811-4 (hc)
ISBN: 978-1-9822-6823-7 (e)

Library of Congress Control Number: 2021908518

Balboa Press rev. date: 04/27/2021

"The dream is the liberation of the spirit from the pressure of external nature, a detachment of the soul from the fetters of matter". – Sigmund Freud

Table of Contents

Message from the Author

· ·

Kristen Andersen, Ed. D

I f you have a passion, your unconscious will reveal the depths of that passion. If you have struggled with the process, your unconscious will release those struggles. If you have enjoyed the success of your efforts, your unconscious will celebrate those successes. Be true to yourself, be true to your passions, and give yourself the allowance to be vulnerable.

Welcome to Unconscious Memories, Volume II, Dream into the Music. This compilation of short stories focuses on dream memories that revolve around the passion for musical expression. What are you passionate about? Are your passions revealed in your dreams? Have you yet to dream of your passion? Have you yet to dream at all? Dreaming is a perplexing experience but, one concept remains reliable, the interpretation of the dream is up to the dreamer. You know the message your unconscious is sending. You know what your dreams indicate. You know why you dream what you dream when you dream it. If you trust yourself, your unconscious mind will reveal an array of insight about who you are, what you do, why you do it, and how that awareness can assist you in your waking life.

Creating the Unconscious Memories series to share my dream memories is one way how I demonstrate my vulnerability and confront my self-realization through a creative lens. As I strive to become a better version of myself, I continue to unleash the most unfiltered cavern of my mind. As I build more knowledge about my dream memories, I grow deeper into comprehending the complex and captivating process of dreaming. So, I continue to write to you vulnerable and amazed by the world of dreams. I continue to write to you bewildered and fascinated by the endless discoveries captured from dream experiences. As I dream into the music with great humility, gratitude, and detail, I write to you, from my unconscious memories.

ASYNCHRONOUS ENSEMBLE

Asynchronous Ensemble

. . . .

Y ou are at a multi-stage beach house party to see your brother and his wife perform some music. Their performance is being evaluated by a wide variety of musician judges. Your mother wants you to look after her car, purse, and other belongings as she leaves to take care of important business. You see a long-lost friend who used to own a fish store. She avoids you by hiding and then walks away. You look around but do not have your glasses. You cannot see everything that is going on. Another friend nicknamed Jon-Jon anxiously points at your long-lost friend and says, "There she is, and she is completely avoiding you". You realize that you left your mother's items in an unattended and unlocked vehicle. You acknowledge what Jon-Jon says and you feel hurt but, you must move on to check on your mother's car and belongings.

Your brother appears and moves the car to a safe spot. As he gets out, he throws you the keys. He wants you to move it to the bottom floor of the house. You get in and move the car. You reach the bottom floor but when you attempt to adjust your parking you create a serious problem. Your mother's car is below what you thought was the bottom level and is stuck in the sand. You are panicking about your mother's belongings and favorite car, so you decide to call her. You begin to dial, but your phone does not work properly. You think it is because you are underground. You realize that it is impossible to turn the vehicle around. There is just not enough room. Strange people in the parking garage stare, yell, and laugh at your predicament. Luckily, a few of them are kind and attempt to help out but, there is nothing anyone can do. You finally get through to speak with your mother on the phone and begin to tell her what happened. Frustratingly, she cannot hear anything you are saying. You lose the call and ring her back several times but, she still cannot hear you. You tell her you will call her back once you get clearer reception.

You are back upstairs at the music performance. The inside looks like a beach house you stayed at a long time ago. You see your brother and his wife on stage. Your father is there in the audience. He sees you, smiles, and waves. You look up to watch their performance but, your old bandmates are hesitant to play. There is a background drumbeat coming from one of the effects pedals. You see them doing well but suddenly begin to struggle. The beat is not in sync. They are unhappy. They are angry. They are beginning to argue on stage. The music is suffering and there is a sloppiness that cannot be covered up. You feel terrible inside. You want so badly to help them, but you know that they do not want you to perform after you left the band so long ago. The audience is mostly silent, but you hear faint whispers about their performance. Your brother and his wife are instructed by the venue to change stages and go to the lower level. You want to follow them to offer support. Your father stays by the main stage. He is sitting in a giant red booth. He knows for certain that they will come back up to perform. You ask him to go downstairs with you, but he is adamant about staying in the booth and repeatedly says that they will return.

You believe your father that they will return, but you also do not want to miss their performance downstairs.

You wait for as long as you can before growing anxious and impatient. You decide to go find them on the lower level. As you make your way, you accidentally bump into an attractive Hispanic man. You ask him, "Where is the music coming from and how do I get there"? He condescendingly tells you, "It is right around the corner and then it will be right in front of your face"! You look at him and frustratingly reply with, "Jeez, I am sorry, I didn't see it and I have never been here before"! As you walk away the guy taps your arm and says, "Oh gosh, hey, I am so sorry, I didn't mean anything bad by it". You are shocked that he becomes kind and sincere. You appreciate his apology but, at the same time are quite confused by his response and question his genuineness.

You finally get to the lower-level performance hall and around the corner is a smaller area with a swimming pool. You see your brother's wife standing in front of the audience. You wonder why she is not on stage. She greets you and says, "Well, hello old friend". You consider not acknowledging the greeting, but you instantly change your mind. You look into her eyes and she does not resemble how you remember. She appears to be shorter, heavier, with larger bright orange eyes, and hair like a pixie. She has changed so much from the last time you saw her. You reply, "Well, hello old friend". You greet her with a hesitant smile but rapidly reach out to hug her. She hugs you back tightly. You both embrace for longer than you expect. You feel the old friendship you once had long ago when you were just teenagers. Both of you are reluctant at first but happy to be connected again after so many years.

You look around and see some of your sister-in-law's family. They stare you down in hatred. They despise you. You do not care about their opinion. You know the truth of your role and how long it has been since the fallout. You look up and recognize your brother on stage. He is playing one of the songs you used to play as a band. He is trying hard and doing the best he can. Unfortunately, the crowd is not responding positively. They are barely considering his performance and appear to be distracted. You begin to grow angry that no one is listening or paying attention to his efforts. Again, you are concerned and want to help him out, but you know he does not want you to perform after you left the band so long ago. Marvelously, the crowd is huge, and the house is packed, but sadly the audience remains unresponsive. You remain frustrated and look around with disdain and desperation. And now, it is just another memory.

Atelier Underground

. . . .

I t is nighttime and quite late. You are in downtown L.A. and trekking the busy streets to get to your destination. You see a variety of people go into this odd, narrow, underground walkway. It resembles a miniature underpass and is hundreds of feet long with openings on both ends that lead to the outside. As you make your way through, there are a bunch of different rooms horizontally aligned to your right and left. You hear a lot of musicians playing instruments and talking about recording. You arrive at the studio. Your sister-in-law answers the door. As you walk in, you see an old bandmate and are very confused about why he is there. Oddly, he is incredibly happy to see you and you greet each other with a hug.

You walk deeper into the studio and see two other people that you have not seen in a while. You are overly excited to greet them. You hug them both in disbelief that they are there. You do not exactly remember who they are, but you know that they are from some point in your life. You have feelings of shock and already think that this get-together is positively awesome and bizarre. Everyone there is a musician! As you look around, you notice that many people are drinking and doing drugs. It seems like everyone is focusing on getting wasted rather than on playing music. You start to get annoyed but contain your irritation. You have a feeling that the abuse will get out of hand, but you ignore it and try to have a good time. You see an all-female band go on stage to perform. They begin to sing some oddly composed acapella songs. Their voices are screeching, shrill, and the lyrics are inaudible. It is a weird performance and even though you are proud of their courage, you do not enjoy the music.

Your youngest maternal uncle shows up and he cannot wait to start playing. You are happy to see him there. He mentions how much he wants to "get on that bass" and rambles on about how he wants to be a "real" musician. As he speaks, there is a sudden shift, and the studio appears to be tiny. Strangely, you notice that the room is automatically expanding as more and more people begin to show up. You also notice that the studio walls are covered in shaggy multi-colored carpet with speckles. You are astonished to see the room growing behind your uncle. You are not sure if the room is getting bigger or if all the drugs in the air are making you hallucinate. Regardless, you continue to hunt for your ukulele that you have been searching for the entire evening. You grow more and more uneasy as you scavenge the studio to find it. You see your sister-in-law and say, "Why didn't you tell me this was going to be about performing? I would have brought my instruments so I could get on stage too". You desperately want to play. You start to feel angry and disappointed. She does not respond to you, so you ask her again more aggressively, "Why the hell didn't you tell me that this was going to be about musical performance so I could have brought my gear"! She ignores you and does not care that you do not have an instrument. She walks away from you and floats around to talk to other people instead.

You finally see your brother. He is jamming on guitar in the back of the room and surrounded by people. He occasionally looks up to chat. Everyone at the studio wants the band reunited to perform again. The four of you are happy to play, but since you do not have an instrument, it cannot happen. You grow even more upset and irritated about the lack of music and all the drug use. You feel left out of everything and you still cannot find your ukulele. The all-female acapella band continues to perform on stage. They are getting intensely loud with their odd voice tricks. They harmonize and arrange intricate tunes. You listen to their band but, the sounds remain unenjoyable. Your youngest maternal uncle comes back into view. He has a giant joint in his hand and is trying to pass it around to everyone. He also has extreme quantities of liquor that he is sharing and telling everyone to "get drunk, y'all"! After he finishes passing all the toxins around, he sits down on the couch next to you. He starts talking about music at first but then he quickly begins to speak garble that is hard for you to understand. You realize how wasted he is and that you will never be able to have a conversation.

At this point, you look around and recognize that the entire party is not about music at all. It is bull****. It is about who can get the highest off of whatever alcohol and drugs are available. You tire of all the random, clamorous, nonsensical conversations. You are antagonized by all of the out-of-tune instruments and high-pitched half-melodies. Inside, you wish you never came to the event. You thought it was going to be about music, but it is certainly not.

You are disturbed by the façade, the charade, the pretense of needing to be high to be a musician. Your sister-in-law and youngest maternal uncle scare you with their advocacy for less music and more partying. The success of the gathering becomes unimportant, and you start to become nonexistent. You deeply recognize that the music is secondary, and you are angry that you wasted your time.

Luckily, your love unexpectedly shows up at the door. They sensed you were unhappy and want you to leave with them. You feel utter relief wash over you. You are more than ready to go. You walk out the door arm in arm through the tapered underpass and head toward what looks like a subway staircase. When you get to the top of the stairs you are in downtown L.A. again. It is still late at night and you are back where you started. You dodge and weave through several people who are walking in a mad rush. You pass by many different vendors selling all types of trinkets and expensive khachkars. The vendors assertively try to sell you stuff that you do not want or need. Regardless of feeling annoyed and unhappy about your surroundings, you and your love walk forward together. Both of you cannot wait to get out of the downtown crowd. Soon, you spot the truck and while you do your best to get closer, you must push through the masses once again. And now, it is just another memory.

Canon in Bowie

· · · · · · · · · · · · · · · · · · · ·

Y ou are at a concert hall and you are sitting next to Bowie. You feel the most amazing feeling you have ever felt in the presence of a musician. Many other well-accomplished players are sitting close by. Young students also surround the seating area mesmerized by the concert. Bowie slings his body from seat to seat, socializing with the audience. Every time he moves, you all stand up. He notices that everyone stands each time his body shifts. He is so happy about the reaction that he cannot help but smile, laugh, and raise his arm in a powerful and approving gesture. He is young and resembles Petty but, everyone knows that he is genuine, Bowie. He has such humble and kind energy. His spirit radiates through the concert hall like the frequency of a deep note vibration on a xylophone. He is willing to speak with anyone and he makes the effort to communicate. You are so excited and privileged to sit with him for the majority of the show.

You notice how large and dark the concert hall appears. You realize that no one is on stage and that music is playing through gigantic theater speakers. You recognize the song. No one could mistake such an epic tune as "Starman". Bowie sits down next to you after making the rounds with more guests and starts talking about music. He utters a few comments and then moves to the seat in front of you. He turns around to ask you questions. You both joke and laugh about bands breaking up. For a moment you both laugh so hard that the entire audience turns their heads to look at the two of you. He continues to talk and encourage you. He tells you that you are talented, to keep playing, and never let go of your ambition.

Meanwhile, there is a drummer with super long curly brown hair that keeps staring at you. You can feel that he likes you. He has been sitting behind you the entire time but finally starts to speak with you. He is making you laugh so hard by telling music jokes. Strangely, he keeps a giant sack with him, and it looks like a bag that Santa Claus would carry. He lets you know that the sack contains all of his music equipment. The bag seems too heavy to schlep around but, he is confident in his strength. Suddenly and with irony, he falls through the gap in the bleacher-style seating and everyone in the audience starts to laugh at him. You feel compassion and without delay, reach your arm down to help. He grabs you and pulls himself up to squeeze back through the bleachers. After you assist him, he seems to become even more attracted and excited about who you are. You can feel that he likes you on another level. Somehow, he discovers that you are a drummer too. He begins to flirt with you even more by complimenting your forearms, touching your shoulders, hugging you, and placing his arms around your waist.

Oddly, another man sitting next to you finds you to be an amazing friend and sparks a joint in your honor. He starts passing it around to everyone in the row. When the joint comes your way, you respectfully decline by saying no thank you. It smells fantastic and you think to yourself, "Wow, I am not even smoking weed in my dreams"? You are shocked by your behavior and for a moment, acknowledge that you are dreaming. After you refuse to partake in the noble herb, the drummer guy likes you even more. He admires that you are staying clean and true to yourself despite the cultural expectations to smoke pot because you are a rock musician at a rock concert. Staying true to yourself turns him on. During the concert, you converse and gain a deeper mental and physical connection with him. He touches your hips, hugs you again, and caresses your arms in admiration of your skill and dedication.

As the evening progresses, you tell him that you are recording an album with your fiancé upstairs. He is dumbfounded that you have a partner and becomes upset. He expresses to you that having a fiancé' is not married and that it is not too late. He still pursues you despite that he is unhappy about the news. You tell him that you need to go back upstairs to finish a few recordings with your love. You leave and as you walk, you swing your body up multiple steps and levels of the concert hall. He watches your every move. He stares and speaks about you to other people. You can hear him complimenting you despite that you are getting further and further away. He talks about your arm strength and your curves. He talks about your creativity and connection with drumming. He says nothing but kind words and you feel confidently flattered.

You arrive upstairs and meet your love. You talk about the album you are creating and speak about the drummer guy with the super long curly brown hair. You mention to your love that he is a famous drummer but, you are not certain what band he is in. You also say that the guy likes you and was hitting on you for half the evening. Your love repeatedly says, "No, no, no, no, no" and gets angry, jealous, and more upset than you ever would have expected. This reaction surprises you because your fiancé is not the jealous type. You are happy about the enviousness because it makes you feel wanted and important. After a few moments, you look at each other and think the entire thing is silly. You both laugh but, are still a little uncomfortable about the situation. You remember that you have to leave the recording room to go pick up a couple of music items downstairs.

As you walk through the theater, you run into the drummer guy again. This time, you see him sitting in front of a lounge room door. He is happy you are there. He begins talking with you about music gigs and electrical positions in the movie industry. He says that he is having a challenging time finding jobs to fund his music projects. He goes on about how many excellent gigs there are in Denver, Colorado. While he is talking, you keep trying to figure out why he is famous. It bothers you that you cannot recall. He tells you that he is going to Denver to play music and that you should go with him. He says he knows a ton of famous bands that would love to have you as their drummer. He reassures you that you could teach and play music out there too. You wonder how true this is since he just expressed that he was having a hard time finding gigs. You begin to think he is only saying these things because you are female, and he wants to get in your pants. He reiterates that he will be touring with his famous band while making money. However, you are confused. You think to yourself, "If he is famous and touring, then why does he need to find a job to fund his music projects"? You revel in the excitement of a possible music opportunity but, are deeply concerned about his motives. You do not trust him. You want to go finish your album with your true love upstairs. Strangely, you see a vision of your fiancé put away a comic book in a closet. And now, it is just another memory.

Crash Performance

. . . .

You are with your love on your way to play a show. You are going to a huge auditorium and you are both extremely excited to perform. Frustratingly, there are too many people on the freeway. The traffic is intolerable. It is a mess. You are trying to get to the venue on time in a tiny hybrid car that looks like your love's parents' vehicle. The freeway is beyond chaotic and the weather is gloomy and drizzling. There are cars everywhere. Suddenly you both see that people are smashing into one another. Your love is dodging and weaving in between the cars and rushing to get to the performance. Multiple wrecks continue to happen in front of you over and over again. Several cars flip, pounce, and explode into terrifying chaos. Other cars are doing 180s and 360s while launching into the air and plowing together mid-flight. You both do the best you can to stay calm while swerving in and out of near death.

For a moment, your time and your vision go into slow motion. You can see the distinctness and detail of every crashing car. You see the wind expand and contract from the vehicles colliding. You see metal parts snap, tires pop, and glass shatter. As you and your love move through the intensity of the crashes you get closer to a freeway off-ramp. Over dozens of vehicles are repeatedly bashing into one another creating a giant pile-up. It is the most reckless and shocking scene. Your love is doing the most impressive job breaking free from the disaster so that both of you do not get hurt. Your love swerves and slows, speeds and merges. Up ahead you see what looks like thousands of cars stacked on top of one another. There is smoke, fire, and broken pieces everywhere. The noise is blaring, and the air is filled with toxins. Every vehicle is in shambles. You speak with each other about how insane the drive is and how grateful you are to be together. You compliment your love on how well they are maintaining. You commend their maneuvering skills and are thankful that they are behind the wheel.

Despite your love's gift for motor vehicle operation, you both worry that you will never make it to the performance. You watch and hold on while your love takes jumps, skids off guard rails, and escapes fatality. There are so many destroyed vehicles on the freeway that it looks like a gigantic junkyard. As you get even closer to the pile-up you see that there is nowhere to go. Your love tries to crisscross but there is no path through the unavoidable destruction. The number of debris is like nothing either of you has ever seen. Luckily, this is the last stretch of insane driving. Your love takes control and says, "F*** it"! The tiny hybrid is pressed to full speed, charges, and plows right over the stacked cars like a monster truck. It skids, slides, and positions sideways right in front of the auditorium. The car is pulverized. There is barely anything left of it after the impact. You are both blessed to be unharmed given the way the car looks. You turn to your love in relief and gratitude. You both feel rapturous to be alive!

You check your internal clock, and you are late for the gig. With all the chaos, you are not surprised that you are not on time. You begin to rush. You get out of the fragmented hybrid and your love tells you that they will meet you inside with the rest of the gear. You are appreciative and head to the performance. You go into the auditorium and it is packed with people. You have tight jeans on, and your sticks are pointing up from your right back pocket. Everyone is waiting and chanting excitedly and impatiently for both of you to get on stage. There are exhilaration and anticipation in the air. Everyone wants to hear the impeccable tunes written by you and your love. The audience is chanting your names. You come through the front even though the fans are not supposed to see you. You are in a rush and there is no way for you to hide so you walk through the auditorium and everyone starts screaming. You exclaim, "Yeah, we made it"! with a smile and a wave while the crowd explodes in joyous celebration.

You make your way backstage and see one of your advisee music college students who drums and sings. She says to you, "S*** boss, you made it! I heard about the car crashes and it sounded crazy. I cannot believe you are here! I just got done performing but, I can go back up there again to buy you time". You reply, "Hell, Yes! Thank you so much! The car is totaled, and the gear is still being unloaded". Your student goes on stage. You settle in to get ready to rock and roll. You tune some drums, speak with a few people, and direct some of your crew to help you get ready. A fellow drummer who looks like Lennon helps with the setup of the kits. He makes sure that everything runs smoothly. You trust him and direct him to get the gear in place. He greets fans, organizes the stage, and makes sure that you are well-prepared for the performance. The audience is intensely screaming, chanting, and the volume becomes deafening. The pressure and suspense are building up to what will be an excellent show. You are ecstatic that you made it! You are ready! The audience is thunderous! You cannot wait for your love to return so you can rock this thing together. And now, it is just another memory.

Marketplace Motif

. . . .

You are in a giant marketplace surrounded by food and music. Tents are set up everywhere. It is the size of 12 city blocks and is built like a maze. The venue has a festival aura, and you feel like you are in another country. Many walls and vendors divide the visually odd environment. You are feeling positive and excited to be there. You know that there will be a lot of opportunities for musical expression, and this fills you with joy. A very skinny lady with curly brown hair is setting up concert booths and arranging the bands. She appears to be the music performance manager. You connect with her and she asks you to go deeper into the maze to get groceries. She tells you to hurry back before the music begins.

You walk through the marketplace and stop at a store. Your mother is there. She is shopping and grooving to the music in the background. You explore the merchandise together and buy the items requested by the manager. A man with two young children starts talking with you and your mother. He is charming and attractive. He gives you the sense that he wants to go out with you. It seems like he will ask for your number, but he never musters the courage. You want to offer to keep in touch but, you do not think it is appropriate since you are in a monogamous relationship. You feel disappointed because he is intriguing, and your mother likes him. As the three of you talk more, you realize you do not like the idea that he has two children. You do not want to be involved in such a complicated situation. You feel relieved by looking at the reality of his and your life. You are happy that you are in a relationship and did not give him your number.

You return to the manager's booth with the groceries. She is shocked that you made it in time. You had your doubts too because you were so caught up speaking with your mother and the man with the children. Despite the manager's doubts, she is dazzled by your fortitude. You are relieved. She thanks you for your services and sends her appreciation through compassionate eye contact. You see a band up on stage and a student you used to know is performing. He looks and acknowledges that you are there. Many people are excited about the band, so they engulf the pit and begin to dance. As the music booms, you go backstage and practice for a little while on guitar. You cannot hear the mainstage anymore but instead, listen to a mini-concert going on in a small back room. Strangely, the room is covered in wood and has amazing acoustics but looks like the architecture at the Whiskey. You will be next to perform a mini-concert.

Before you take the stage, you need to use the restroom. As you enter, you see that it is filthy. There are several portable toilets filled with urine and excrement. There is so much disgustingness that there is no place for you to pee. Another girl is there, and she looks at you and says, "How the f*** are we supposed to pee in here? I am not peeing in here, this is nasty"! You look at her and without a doubt, agree. You are so sickened by the sight that you lose the urge to use the bathroom. You both flee the grotesque scene.

You go back to the marketplace where the music is booming! You weave your way through the crowd to get back to where you started. You see a variety of musicians talking, laughing, tuning instruments, and getting ready to jam. The marketplace is covered in people. It is the busiest that you have seen it since you arrived. As you make your way through the crowd, a vendor has a signed copy of an album from a metal band that you are known for hating. There is also a deal where you can meet the band if you buy the album. The signed copy is really rare and special. You try to look at the album, but the vendor will not let you until you agree to meet the band. You become confused by the stipulation, grow distracted, and disregard the vendor's proposition. You are glad to move on because you need to get back to the mini-concert stage. You weave your way through the audience and vendor booths that are filled with instruments and merchandise. You pass a poster on the wall of an attractive woman's face. You like the energy of the woman. You begin to have a crush on her. You want to meet her, but it is only a poster, and you feel absurd.

As you walk past the rock and roll vendors selling t-shirts, you feel rushed to get back to play guitar. You see various items for sale, but you cannot slow down to shop because you have to perform soon. As you forge through the insane amount of stuff, you see your brother from afar. You are amazed that he is there. He is working on something musical and looks up at you with pure elation. You are overjoyed to see him filled with contentment. You wave at him with a beaming smile. He waves back at you with a large, gleaming, white-toothed grin. You can feel that he is delighted to see you, and this fills you with peace. You do not stop to speak to each other. You know that words do not matter. You are both cloaked in so much musical triumph. You make your way to the mini-concert stage with positive vibration and elevated ambition. And now, it is just another memory.

Monks Hymn

. . . .

T housands of people are gathered in a gigantic concert hall. The audience members are sitting on the floor and backed away about 10 feet from the platform. They are in awe of the musical performances. You are overwhelmed that you have the opportunity to hear music made by monks. You feel honored to listen to the hymns and cannot believe you are there. You are beyond grateful to be backstage. You have a feeling that you might perform but, are at peace with being a spectator. Surprisingly, one of the eldest monks who is known for his strict, pleasant, and disciplined disposition calls you to the stage. Your feeling is correct.

He wants you to perform with him. You are shaken by your prediction and reluctant to oblige because you have never played music with him in front of an audience. You are excited but frightened. You are nervous but overjoyed. You are appreciative but hesitant. You do not know if you will be able to play as well as he requires.

You and the monk go on stage to sit on separate custom-made rugs. As you take your seats, you face one another. Placed in front of you are hand drums that look similar to bongos. You start to feel the monk's purpose and intent for the music. You begin to hear the rhythms inside his head. As you sense what he sees, you start to play the beats on the drums. As he hears your progression he begins to chant. He sends you vibrations of what he wants you to play, and you play it. You are in sync with him. You are in tune with his thoughts. The more you both connect, the better you perform. Neither of you utters a word. There is no need to speak. You occasionally look into one another's eyes but otherwise, you unify unseen. For a moment you glance at your drums and at the audience filled with monks and laypeople sitting motionless and mindful in the gigantic concert hall.

Your initial hesitation and nervousness have melted away. All the thoughts of not being good enough have dissipated. Your musical-spiritual partner has made you feel comfortable and confident. You will dynamically close this show together as a team. He sends you waves of admiration from his mind and heart unto yours. Through your collaboration, you capture the beats he foresees you to play. As you repeatedly let go and feel the merge with the monk, you progressively get better and know you are capable of flawlessness. You feel your hands getting faster. The monk is chanting louder and more intentionally. You look down. Your hands are so swift that everything is blurry. The lightning speed at which you are delivering sound skews the definition of your digits. Your hands become one with the drums. Your every hit matches every note of his voice and every note of his voice connects to every nerve ending in your fingertips. Your spirits are intertwined through the frequencies.

The audience remains silent, mindful, and motionless. You can feel that they are in a state of reverence. As the mantra ends, your timing exceeds anything you have ever played. Your belief in yourself supported by the monk's belief in your ability strengthens your technique. After the performance concludes everyone in the audience explodes in an uproar of exuberance. They applaud, they whistle, they scream. You feel all the positive energy radiate through your body. The audience's reaction is full of pure love for the two of you. You both glow with admiration for one another. Now that the show has ended, the audience begins to leave, the musicians begin to pack up, and all of the close family, friends, and fans come onto the stage to congratulate their loved ones. Everyone is rejoicing and you can feel yourself illuminate.

Your brother is there and the first person to come up to you. He hugs you tight and says, "Hey, you looked a little nervous up there but, you did amazing, were you nervous"? You reply, "Yeah, I was a little bit nervous at first but, then I was fine, thank you for being here". Before you can fully acknowledge the conversation, your brother disappears. Your love comes up on stage next and gives you the longest and tightest hug. The embrace is so overwhelming and emotional. Your eyes fill up with tears. As your love hugs you, you hear a whisper in your ear, "I am so proud of you. I am just so proud of you". You kiss. The pressing of your lips is so soft, pure, and sweet that you forget where you are and why you are there. You grab each other's hand to hold while looking into each other's eyes. Then, your mother makes her way to the stage with tears streaming down her face. She is overwhelmed by your connection with the monk. She is impressed by your power to overcome your nervousness. She appreciates the demonstration of your passion. She looks at you, smiles, and shakes her head in positive approval. The only shake of a head that a mother can give when in such a state of pride and incredulity.

Lastly, your performance partner, the amazing monk, comes over and puts his hand on your left shoulder. You turn around and meet his eyes with yours. He stares at you with an effervescent grin while his face begins to glow a shiny golden yellow. He glows so brightly that you can feel his every emotion. All his joy. All his pride. All his peace. He assures you that you are capable of more. He encourages you to pursue your path. He needs you to keep believing in yourself. He needs you to be even greater than flawless. You wonder what is greater than flawless. He smiles and looks into your eyes. You gaze back and smile with humility. And now, it is just another memory.

Musical Butterfly

· · · · · · · · · · · · · · · · · · · ·

Y ou are starting a new college and it is orientation day. You are stylishly dressed and thrilled to begin this new chapter in your life. You know that this is one of the most elite music schools in the country. The sun is shining bright, and the college is the size of a small high school. You are confused and uncertain about what grade you are in. There are students and parents everywhere. There is a lot of competition to get accepted. You come into the college as a drummer, but every band needs a guitarist. You think this is so weird because the world is filled with excellent guitarists. Luckily, you are carrying your brother's old Yamaha that was passed to him by your father. You love this guitar. You have had it for many years, and it is a deep part of your musical soul. With your strings strapped to your back, you look around the college and tour the halls.

You see a few memorable faces from your elementary school but, in particular a boy who used to make fun of your weight. You are in the same classroom as him. He is practicing his instrument and both of you are auditioning for the same parts. You are excited to be there despite feeling extremely shy about your performance skills. The classroom is exceptionally loud. Everyone is playing instruments and talking about their personal lives. You practice through the noise to get over being shy. You notice that there are a few instructors who do not like you. Their body language signals that they think you are musically incapable of succeeding at this school.

One instructor, in particular, despises you. She is from a high-class Austrian musical background. She does not feel that you have what it takes to be a publicly accomplished musician. She wants to hold you back from attending. She is not kind to you. She bosses you around and insults you throughout the entire orientation. She tells you what you can and cannot do. She says that you will never be a better musician if you do not change everything you think you know. She tells you that you are not talented. She is rude. She is cruel. You hate her. Sadly, you begin to believe the disparaging commentary. You are not good enough. You need to look better, dress better, act better and perform better. You will never make a positive impression no matter what you do. You lack confidence and feel left behind.

Regardless of being treated like a second-rate human being without any talent, you muster the conviction to head to another classroom to demonstrate your skills. You have been judged as a drummer since you got there even though you will be performing on guitar. You think this is odd. You are asked to sit in the middle of a circle surrounded by multiple observers. Teachers, parents, students, and administrators await your performance. You start playing several old songs on the Yamaha. You are told to use a specific board to decipher the music, but you play by ear to find every note. A male instructor is impressed with your ability to use sound as your guide. He writes comments, shows interest, and compliments you by whispering to another teacher that you are unique. However, since you are unlike the trained musicians in the potential future class, he cannot disclose his desire to recruit you. You are considered a pariah of musicianship at this school and it would be unprofessional for him to acknowledge such an uneducated player. You do not worry about this and instead, let your confidence soar through the Yamaha. You play harder, louder, and more precisely to show off your passion and natural capability.

After you finish your performance, you go outside to the main courtyard. It is spacious and there is an extraordinarily beautiful grassy area set back from the building. The area is bright green with numerous trees and gorgeous blooming flowers. The environment is clean and comfortable. There are white circular tables and chairs for visitors to sit and eat with their loved ones. Students, parents, and instructors are scattered all over. Tables are set up with food and drink for everyone to enjoy. There are many multi-colored balloons to commemorate the process of orientation. An enormous and breathtaking tree sits in the middle of the campus courtyard. It catches your attention. It is so unbelievably stunning that you stop to acknowledge its beauty. Once you admire the magical tree, you walk around to look for a place to relax.

You see your mother. She is late but, wanting to visit with you. As she walks down a flight of stairs you recognize that she is unhealthily thin. However, she is dressed like a classy, upscale businesswoman and has the attitude to match. Her confidence is beaming despite looking sickly. She is excited to explore the campus and mingle. You see her speak with a few parents. She is conversing and laughing happily in their company. After socializing she makes her way through the grassy area of the campus. She wants you to go to her. You give her a big hug and both of you walk through the beautiful courtyard together. You stop to look at the enormously breathtaking tree. It is something out of a fairy tale. She points out the many colorful flowers growing from the tree branches. You have never seen anything like it before. Your mother is moved by its enchantment. As both of you gaze at the perplexing nature of the tree, you see a massive butterfly. It must be at least 5 feet long and 3 feet wide! It is purple, light blue, and has highlights of yellow through its wings. You and your mother are amazed and stop to stare.

You do not want to scare it away. You stand back and appreciate its majesty.

Suddenly, a rush of students and parents start running and colliding into one another to get closer to the tree. They are trying to catch the butterfly. More people join the crowd and begin to frighten the stunning Lepidoptera. One lady grabs what looks like a 10-foot long flower stalk and pokes at the magical creature. The butterfly is terrified and curls up tightly. The crowd of impatient and disrespectful people loudly heckle the shuddering wonder. The noise scares the phenomenal living artform into a panic. It flutters and flies from one flower branch to another and then another. It is trying to stay safe and get away from the swats and grasps of the human mob that is attempting to capture it. You are upset and disgusted with everyone's behavior. Your mother is in disbelief about what she is seeing. You cannot understand why they would want to frighten and harm such an alluring being. This unfortunate incident changes your mind about the school. You do not want to go there, and you cannot wait to leave. You and your mother have had enough and agree that this is not the place for you. As you exit the campus together, you look back at the tree, and the butterfly is gone. And now, it is just another memory.

Ocean Studio

· · · · · · · · · · · · · · · · · · · ·

Y ou go to see your brother at his studio. The place is very strange. It is shaped like a fairground with booths on the sand and the ocean is 5 feet away. The floor is made of grass and the waves surround the area. You go under a tent that looks like an awning and you see your brother sitting at a cubicle. In front of him is a long brown foldable table typically used to place food at parties. On top of the table is some music equipment and what looks like the old desktop computer that your father used to have in the 90s. With the ocean water breaking so close to the tent, you wonder why your brother is working in such a bizarre space.

Despite the constructs of the studio, you are happy that you can finally sit down and speak to each other without arguing. You both want to talk about what happened to the band and the business. Each of you expresses your thoughts and feelings peacefully for the first time and it is a relief after being so misunderstood for so many years. Without distraction, you can finally connect with your brother. You hash out everything about the business. You talk specifically about why it ended the way it did. As you begin to think that things are getting better, the communication starts to get volatile. He is angry, upset, and starts to yell. You become angry and begin to yell too.

After a while, things calm down and he sits back in his chair to do a few things on the computer. He mentions that he is struggling with the business and that you are at fault. You do not understand the blame because it has been so many years since you were involved. You continue to explain why you left but, he does not want to hear it. You try and express to him that you were both equally frustrated when working together. You reassure him that it was the best thing for both of you. You remind him how much you were not getting along. You tell him that he felt judged and nagged while you felt used and unappreciated. You reiterate that neither of you agreed with how the business was being run. You explain again why you chose to take yourself out of the picture. He goes back and forth with agreeing and disagreeing while understanding and not understanding. You explain that you were the one who left with nothing but your drum kit. He still does not see your reality even though he has the equipment, the studio, and the business to prove his success. You tell him that you are proud of him and everything he has accomplished. He grows quiet and sits back in his chair again. He has a look of contemplation on his face as a wave breaks closer to the tent-covered studio.

As you stand in the grass, a new business partner of your brothers with a similar last name arrives. He has blondish-red medium-length hair that is pulled back in a ponytail. He is stocky, wears a baggy t-shirt with long beige cargo shorts, and is drinking a bottle of pop. He sits at a cubicle across from your brother. You can tell that he is pretending to work while eavesdropping on your conversation. You and your brother start to argue about the business again and you begin to raise your voice. You are so angry that you cannot get along. You begin to fight even more. Your brother's new business partner feels the need to interrupt. He repeatedly states that it is all your fault and everything you did had no reasoning. You reply with disgust and rage by saying, "And who the f*** are you, man? Get the f*** out of here, so I can speak with my brother because this has absolutely nothing to do with you"! He replies by scornfully saying, "Well, you haven't even been around in 4 years so what do you care"? You respond with even more disdain, "My brother hasn't been around me either, the story goes both ways jerkoff, and we are trying to work it out together so why don't you go and f*** off, so I can talk with my brother"! He finally shuts up, grabs his pop, and walks out of the studio tent cubicle. Your brother is unphased by your aggression toward his colleague and randomly wants to show you a video he created.

In the video, your brother is imitating an ace comedian from your childhood. You would never expect your brother to imitate any comedian or perform as anything other than a musician. The video is supposed to be funny, but you do not laugh. You are shocked and wonder why he would use his time like this. Regardless, your brother is happy about it and you support his endeavor with a reassuring smile. After the video is over, your brother tries speaking with you more about the business and how it ended. He wants to talk about missing documents, but you tell him that there are not any. Your brother grows angry and thinks you are hiding them. You repeatedly tell him that you do not have what is talking about. As you explain that you would never hide anything from him, the wet documents wash up from an incoming wave and onto the grass floor of the studio. Your brother looks down, acknowledges the documents, and relaxes in his chair once again.

Suddenly, the new business partner texts your brother. "I am sorry you are having such an issue with your sister but, I am always here for you, I am your friend, and I am never going to leave. I am not like your family and I am never going to abandon you as your family did"! You know what the text says because your brother reads it out loud to you. As he reads the text, multiple waves crash onto the grass floor of the studio. The tent poles begin to shake, and the waves start to damage your brother's equipment. Your brother looks at you with intense worry. You look at your brother in silence. There is nothing more you can say for him to understand, believe, or know that you care. The only way to unite is to take action. You and your brother start moving the instruments and electronics into a black SUV as fast as possible. As the studio begins to fill up with water, you both rush and hustle to keep everything safe. You never speak about the band. While the waves impedingly crash, you work together to save all the gear. And now, it is just another memory.

Organized Time

. . . .

You are a teacher and a student at a college that is equally focused on music and academia. You stand on a grassy knoll that has a beautiful music building on top of it. Everyone is playing and performing. You are loving the experience of jamming on the bongos and congas. The small community of musicians is full of life and you do not want to stop playing even though you have a meeting at 11 am. You begin to feel anxious because you are worried about time. You have a terrible feeling that you will be fired. The urgency stops you from playing percussion. On your way to the meeting, you run into Grohl and start chatting. You are not surprised that he is there. It is as if you have always known him. Grohl tells you that you have a unique style and that you can make it. His band is playing in the background and he tells you to go join. You have zero hesitation. You get on the drum kit and start rocking out with the band. He gets on guitar and you both begin to groove. Numerous people gather around and clap. You know that this is where you are supposed to be.

Through the crowd, you see your brother. He comes close to the stage and wants to talk. You are happy to see him, so you leave the jam session and walk over. You start speaking with one another and it briskly turns into an argument. He is upset and unhappy. Your brother screams at you and your sister-in-law appears, interrupts, and tries to speak with him. The conversation between the two of them also turns into an argument. They begin to yell at one another. You are not sure what the fighting is about, but you want to put an end to it. Unfortunately, they do not hear you. You start to get incredibly stressed out. You look back at the grassy knoll and all the musicians and instruments are gone. You are so disappointed that you cannot go back. You remember that you need to get to your meeting on time, but you do not have the necessary paperwork. You have to go to your dorm to get it and do not have much time to talk if you want to make it by 11 am. You tell your brother and sister-in-law that you must go because you cannot be late for this meeting. Your brother angrily looks at you and says, "I have no idea what job you do, I know nothing about you, and it is not my fault that you are going to be late"! You look at your watch and it is 11 am.

You run down the grassy knoll and into a building to get back to the dorms. You sprint through numerous corridors to get closer to the necessary paperwork. You forget all about the fight you had with your sibling and think you overslept your meeting because of your recent surgery. Frighteningly, the dorms are an unbelievably unstable place. You walk into an unending hoarded state of dishevelment. There are students and small children everywhere. The environment is a confusing disaster. The maze of dorms is so aggravating. You cannot find your way around. You head down a huge flight of stairs and see a variety of clustered and unsanitary living rooms. A student you once taught is there and repeatedly tells you to, "Move on b****"! She is so rude to you that you burst into tears and start to panic. Your head is spinning in the anxiety-ridden surroundings. You are overwhelmed by the chaos. You cry profusely but try to get help from a lady in the dormitory. She appears to be the manager but, is impatient and cruel. She looks like a prison warden. She wears dark-squared glasses, a pencil skirt, and carries herself with derogatory masculinity. You ask her where room number 805 is located.

Luckily, she guides you back to your dorm room. You tell her that this is the worst college experience that you have ever had. She looks at you with disdain and expresses zero compassion. You cry uncontrollably. You look around your room and see all of your items scattered everywhere. You cannot find a single thing. Nothing is organized. You are searching for the paperwork, but it is mixed in with art supplies, books, clothes, and tons of other random papers. Heaps and piles inundate your search. Finding anything is not going to happen. You are so stressed out from the disarray. Everywhere in the dormitory is tumultuous. Many people are fighting and yelling in the background. You give your attention to the arguing and it stresses you out even more. You try to speak with your colleagues on the phone to let them know that you will not make it on time. To your misfortune, the call has terrible reception, and the sound keeps breaking up as you talk. You have missed your meeting just like you feared. There is nothing you can do about it. Your job, your money, your time is lost. And now, it is just another memory.

Serenading Guitarist

· · · · · · · · · · · · · · · · · · · ·

You are wearing a tight black dress, black heels, and feeling exceptionally good about yourself. Your body is completely different than you remember. Your make-up looks incredible, and your hair is shoulder-length and straightened. You are about to give a guitar performance on a cruise ship. The ship looks smaller than normal and appears to be a hybrid between a houseboat and a yacht. The kitchen is filled with a variety of drinks and different combinations of food. There are other performers including your old friend from high school and another girl named Frida who resembles a familiar Mexican American actress.

All of you are wearing stunningly simple and matching outfits. There are many older people in the audience ready to see the show. You look out and spot your love smiling within the crowd and wearing a shiny black tux. Your mother is there too. She looks classy in a black dress, feather boa, and is covered in diamond jewelry.

You finally take the stage. You perform and sing with robust vibrance. You are thrilled to be playing music and love that this is your life. It is a gorgeous starry night with a light breeze that is embracing and smells intoxicating. You are invigorated by the atmosphere. The audience is receptive, and you are so pleased that they are enjoying the music. You see the wait staff serving food and drinks to all the guests. You smile and breathe out each note as you strum your guitar. You know that you have serenaded your life with purpose. You envelope yourself with respect and recognition. As the concert comes to a close, all you can think about is performing again. You have two more nights aboard the ship to share your most cherished songs and you cannot wait. You know that this is where you are meant to be.

You leave the stage and immediately take off your make-up because it is starting to bother your complexion. You apply make-up remover while you relax on a recliner.

You do not care that people are watching because you must get the toxins off of your skin. It was a great look for the show but now, it is time to be natural. After the make-up is off, you look in a hand mirror and see that your face is swollen. Your mother comes up to you and questions your judgment. She does not think it is the appropriate place or time to remove your cosmetics. She does not seem to care that your face is swollen until you explain to her that the make-up has irritated your skin. She listens and looks at you. She sees the swelling and agrees that you did the right thing. As you continue to relax on the recliner, there is a little brown dog that trots over to you. It looks like your first family dog, Murray. You pet the little guy and then he scurries around the deck of the ship. Subsequently, a few people come up to speak with you. A group of beautiful women and a kind-eyed man ask if it is okay to take some utensils, leftover food, and drinks from the kitchen. You tell them to help themselves and feel free to take whatever they want.

You get up off the recliner and walk over to the ship railing. A relatively young, big, and tall man with shaggy hair and black glasses walks over to you. He says that his name is Paul and wants to have a conversation. Unfortunately, he is not your buddy Paul that you used to work with. Although, the name triggers you to think of your buddy and wish that he were there instead. You look over and see that this strange Paul smokes and drinks heavily which makes you not want to talk with him. However, he says that he is a photographer, and it makes you think that you could have some awesome photos taken of you and the other performers at the next gig. He mentions that he does other work, but he will not tell you what it is. You think this is secretive and weird. From across the ship, your love sees you speaking with the strange Paul and gets extremely jealous. You find this to be odd because your love never gets jealous. It is obvious that the guy is flirting with you but, you do not give him the time of day. You are not the least bit interested. You are so very much in love, with your love. Awkwardly, the strange Paul and your love are standing together at the railing of the ship. You walk over and the three of you attempt to communicate but eavesdropping on other people's conversations is all you can do.

Eventually, you stand alone at the ship railing. You look out onto the deck at the other ladies who performed. They are relaxed and filled with gratitude. You think about their beauty, talent, and success. You are so proud of them. You joyfully look around at the many people sitting and socializing while they delight in the remaining food and drinks. You feel the cool ocean breeze against your skin. You pick up the hand mirror again and see that the swelling is gone. Your complexion is glowing and sparkling from the light of the stars flickering off the ocean waves. You look up at the crescent moon. You hear the music in the background and smile. You feel more than content. You feel more than positive. You are perfectly at peace. And now, it is just another memory.

Stolen Pedal

. . . .

Y ou are at a college in a music performance hall.
You go up a flight of stairs with your mother
to celebrate an Easter music festival. There are
lots of girls walking around and everywhere you look
there is a ridiculous amount of chocolate bunnies for
sale. People are loading up and chomping down on these
incessantly awful smell-good treats. One girl leads you
further upstairs to check out more merchandise. She is
talking to you about sugar-covered popcorn and other
unhealthy snacks. She offers you indigestible goodies.
You thank her but tell her that you cannot eat any of it.
She tells you that it is your loss and that you are missing

out. You are bothered by her response and expeditiously dismiss her uneducated commentary.

You and your mother go up the next flight of stairs. The third floor of the performance hall is somehow the worst. When you get to the top, there is an outside area filled with tables covered in holiday decorations. Several student musicians and their families are celebrating. Stuffed Easter bunnies line the tables, chairs, and drapes. You and your mother have never seen so many bunny-themed knickknacks. There are also too many drinks and too much food. You look around and cannot believe that there are so many sweets in one place. There is every variety of chocolate Easter bunny. Hollow, dark, white, solid, crunch, milk, if you can think it, you can eat it! You cannot believe your eyes. As you both take a closer look, you see that most of the Easter bunnies have either been bitten or half-eaten and then left all over the tables. It looks shameful. What seemed to be an extravagant but possibly delightful scene quickly turned into a sloppy and disgusting heap. You both look around and see that people are stuffing themselves. The way that everyone appears while eating this garbage is making you sick. You are so glad that neither of you is part of this repulsive demonstration of gluttony.

You walk to find a clean and empty table. As you and your mother sit down, you meet a dark-haired, dark-eyed, olive skin Italian man. He is moderately attractive and seems to be kind. He gives you a feeling that he is interested in you and sits down at your table without being invited. He begins to speak about your upcoming cholecystectomy. You wonder how he knows about your surgery. Then, he starts talking about music being a wonderful gift. He talks a lot. When you finally get a chance to speak, his body language suggests that he does not care about what you have to say. He does not listen. He repeatedly looks around and is not considerate. He seemed like a decent person at first but, now he is an annoying nuisance. You sense that he has ulterior motives. Luckily, your mother orders some healthy food to the table. It arrives and you can finally eat! You feel relieved. You hope that this deplorable human being will go away so you can dine in peace. Eventually, he leaves after you and your mother ignore him, abandon the food, and decide to go back downstairs to listen to the live music.

Once you get to the bottom floor you make your way to the performance hall. It looks like the old high school theater where your maternal aunt used to put on dance shows when she was an instructor many years ago. Your mother goes and sits somewhere else while you take a seat next to a random guy in the back. You are excited because you will be performing on your kit soon. You just bought this badass kick pedal, and you cannot wait to use it in your performance. You keep it in your backpack so as not to lose or scratch it. You hold onto your stuff as you sit and watch the variety of entertainment. You see your mother sitting on the floor listening to the other bands. She looks over at you, points to her right, and says, "Hey look, how awesome, your brother and his wife are here"! You look over and they are sitting up against the wall. They are quite a distance away. Your brother never looks over at you, but your sister-in-law does. She catches your eye and gives you a piercing stare. She looks at you with pure hatred. Her gaze makes you so uncomfortable that you have to look away. You feel disturbed. You wish that you did not have to deal with them. You wish that they were not there. You never look back again.

You decide to get up from your seat and move around. You leave your backpack and jacket safely under your chair. As you head out to where more snacks are being sold, a man is standing by a winding staircase next to an

ATM just outside the performance hall. You remember meeting him before but, you cannot recall where you were. You lock eyes with him and instantly connect. You like him and he likes you. You walk over to speak with him. You notice he is from another country, has a definitive accent, a scruffy beard, is shorter than you, and is incredibly kind. He asks you many music-related questions and you answer all of them. You find out that he is a jazz guitarist, and he reminds you of a conductor on a series that takes place in the jungle. You never want him to know that you and your mother spoke with the guy upstairs. You are ashamed that you gave such a disingenuous person your time. You stand next to each other and discuss your plans for future shows. It is excellent conversing with him. You wish you could speak with him longer, but you have to go perform. You tell him that you would like to see him later. He says that he will happily listen to you play and he hopes to see you afterward.

You make your way into the theater and sit down. Then you realize that you are not in the same spot where you were sitting before. You get up with a feeling of doom and search for a while but eventually make your way back to your original seat. As you sit down, you check under your chair. You see your backpack and your jacket but, your pedal is missing. While you search under other seats nearby, you hear the audience heckling the bands on stage. They yell and scream, "Amateurs! Losers! Get off the stage"! You feel so bad for your fellow performers. All you can think of is that their courage does not deserve such ridicule. You are embarrassed for the hecklers because they have no morale. You rummage and search for your pedal, but you cannot find it. It is gone. You fill with disappointment. You will not be part of the show. And now, it is just another memory.

Troubled Cymbals

. . . .

Y ou walk into a peculiarly elongated pizza parlor. You see a colossal stage and an exponentially massive crowd. Your father, mother, and anyone you can remember is there to lend support. You are going to be performing tonight. You will play some tunes with your old band but, you have not rehearsed. You have not played drums in years. It has been so long since you played music that you are uncertain why you are even playing a show. Your bandmates are setting up their gear and the lead singer of your love's old band is setting up the drum kit for you. You get on stage, see his work, and he has done such a superficial job that you have to redo everything. You wish you would not have listened to your bandmates. Only you should have set up your kit.

The three toms are tuned and ready to rock but you are having serious problems with the cymbals. As you fix one cymbal, another falls. As you get all the cymbals set up, they all come crashing down. You are trying to balance the kit back and forth to make it work. Oddly, you have cymbals as small as the palm of your hand. As you begin to position them onto the kit, one completely breaks off, and the other flies across the parlor. As you get deeper into the problem, you see that some cymbals are set up so far away that you cannot hit them. You become frustrated and embarrassed that nothing is working. You keep trying to rearrange them the best you can but, the organization and placement are all wrong.

Your father rushes to the stage to help. He is doing the best he can to assist you by tightening the cymbals onto their stands. With an unfortunate defeat, the pressure from the sticks collapses them again. The cymbals are imbalanced and as you hit the left, the right falls, and as you hit the right, the left falls. Your father tries to catch them as you play but, it is much too difficult. He feels bad for you but is powerless to make the cymbals work. It is devastating. Everyone wants to hear the band play and there is nothing you can do. The continuous disappointment of the equipment makes you feel like a failure. Your entire set time has been taken over by never-ending maintenance of cymbals that will not repair.

You look down at the kit and see everything wobbling, but also notice that there is a new issue with the snare. The stand for the snare drum is way too large. You cannot properly tighten the side grips for the snare to stay in place. Every time you try to hit the snare it ends up sliding down the stand. This is extremely problematic and the process to fix everything becomes even more debilitating. You feel useless and your spirit is more broken than the drum kit. You continue to struggle. You rip down parts off the kit and put new parts up. Inevitably, everything breaks over and over again. Your bandmates repeatedly start and stop songs to see if you can manage to play with the defective instrument. You are unsuccessful. The music suffers because of you. Your misery and stress become inordinate.

The audience begins to chant the band's name. You feel the pressure of expectation. Without viable drums, how will you perform? Your bandmates focus on you and wait with distressed faces. They feel bad for your hardship and long for your victory. They are proud of your tenacity but, are discouraged by your ineptitude. They blame the venue for saying that there was a decent house kit. They regret you not bringing your Ludwig. The crowd gets louder and louder with chants for all of you to perform. You feel even more constrained. It is an impossible process as you wrestle with cymbal solidification. Everyone wants to hear you again but, you become the despondency. You never manage to get the kit to work. You never manage to entertain as a band. And now, it is just another memory.

Vibrato Ballroom

. . . .

You are in a tri-floored hotel, ballroom, concert hall. It is a Sunday, and you know that because you wrote it down. You are wearing an enchanting flowy gown that sparkles when you walk. You feel good about the evening and what will come to pass. You are meeting your mother there to spend time with her. You know that your father and the band will be there too. All of you are going to celebrate with one another at this special musical event. You see your band arrive and begin to commemorate the evening. They are sitting at a glass table covered in mini wooden instruments. They are cheerful and throwing their arms up in merriment. Your father walks in and beams with support. He smiles and waves while he speaks with your mother. You are so grateful that they are there. You can hear music going on in the background and wonder who could be performing.

With great misfortune, the joyous feelings of connected parents and an awesome band fade when you see your extended maternal family. You quickly become miserable. You feel like your night is ruined. While you start to notice the effects of the many alcoholic drinks that you never actually drank, you yell at your uncle-godfather for being there. When you finish with your rant, you swiftly walk away from him and select your next target. Your youngest maternal uncle is 10 feet tall and is standing in the background looking much older than you remember. You go up to him and direct an ear-piercing scream. You tell him how selfish and ignorant he is and that you expected more from him. He tries to grab you by the arm, but you wail, shove, and reach up to excessively pound your fists on his chest.

After lashing out at both your maternal uncles, you figure you should go to the bathroom to collect yourself. You walk past a circular bar in the concert lounge. When you get inside the restroom you do not see any doors on the stalls. You look around and the place is squalidly horrifying. You yell, "This is utter bull****"! You turn around to leave but look back to check if the bathroom is any cleaner. Unfortunately, nothing changes. Surprisingly, you catch two girls sitting together on one of the grimy toilets. You cannot believe that they are making out and masturbating. Their actions do not bother you. You like that they are enjoying each other. However, you cannot understand why they would choose such a polluted place to be sexual. You are sickened by their choice of environment and wish they would go somewhere hygienically safe. You are disturbed, disoriented, and never get the opportunity to use the bathroom.

As you make your way through the hall, you are drunk and wobbly. Your steps are skewed, and your vision is blurry. You get closer to the ballroom tables and see your bandmate eating and enjoying her time! You think about what an excellent person she is and how much you love her. Shortly after your admiration, you see your advertising aunt across the table. She starts speaking negatively about the ballroom, the food, and the "this", and the "that". You lose your patience and yell at your aunt. You tell her how spoiled she is and that she has no appreciation or gratitude. You speak in a blaring tone and say, "Stop taking advantage"! as you walk away from the table.

While you continue to feel upset and irritated that your extended maternal family has ruined the evening, you run into your step-grandfather. You feel a wave of heightened emotional anger and resentment. You take one look and decide it is best to ignore him. You know that if you acknowledge his presence that you will choke him to death. You feel ashamed of your thoughts and actions, so you get up and wander the ballroom in your sparkling flowy gown. As you wander, you cry. You think about love and how you have none. None from romance and none from family. You try to separate yourself from the negative feelings and disappointments of the evening. Your attempt is ineffective. You grapple with your emotions as you proceed with your tears.

You walk and you sulk. A man sees you pace and contemplate. He acknowledges that you have been crying and are distressed. Fortuitously, this man manages the circular bar in the concert lounge that you passed on the way to the bathroom. He is handsome, endearing, and hails you down to come to sit at one of the bar stools. He asks you, "Well, how are you"? You timidly say, "I am good, no, I am terrible, no, I will be okay". He smirks and says, "Are you sure about any of that? Is there anything I can do for you"? You cherishingly reply with, "Thank you for being so kind, but no, I will be fine". You know that the man demonstrates the utmost compassion. His simplistic words are enough for you. His facial expressions and the look in his eyes speak volumes about how much he cares for your well-being. He has a special way about him. You feel grateful for this moment. You are uplifted and decide to keep walking through the ballroom.

You hear the music playing. You are so curious about who is performing on stage. You cannot seem to find anyone who knows. While you are walking on the red velvet carpet that lines the entire ballroom floor, you see many people dressed in their dazzling outfits. All of the fashionable guests are dining, drinking, and talking. You even see people gaming and gambling in the hotel casino. Strangely, as you stroll you spot your grey purse sitting in the middle of the walkway. You are unsure how it got there. You are relieved that you have found it even though you forgot about it until now. Nevertheless, you pick it up and throw it over your shoulder. You carry on with your walk and take in your surroundings. As you curiously pursue who is the band you drunkenly slide down a flight of stairs.

You end up on the main floor facing the concert stage where you see the most famous rock band of all time! Now you know who has been playing the music! It is your father's favorite band! Three of the original members are there! You cannot believe they are the ones who have been playing music the entire night! It is so surreal. You spot a new vocalist! He looks like a radio host that your band knows but his hair is much longer. You cannot believe he is singing on stage! You are excited and move closer to the music. Somehow, you end up backstage watching the performance. You are standing by a curtain and see the band's drummer to your right. You are crouching on the ground as to not disturb. You see a streamline of chairs for the top musician attendees. The seats line the sides of the stage like artwork on a wall.

As you watch in awe, the guitarist, bassist, and radio show host come up to you with a microphone. They ask you your name and you eagerly reply. The entire ballroom is focused on you. The three men start asking you drum questions. You respond with the wittiest and stealthiest of answers. They mention that their sons are learning how to play drums. You are so honored to be questioned and feel extremely confident. They ask if you would not mind reading some notes. Before you can respond, a note-covered piece of paper floats in the air toward you. You grab and look at it. You tell them that you cannot read it, but you are more than happy to feel it. They look at you in shock and agreement.

With great warmth, they all give you high-fives, huge hugs, and bring you to the stage. They point at you to get on the drums. You cannot believe you are on stage with them. You are saturated with jubilation and jam as you have never jammed before. You feel valued. You feel humbled. You feel worthy. The performance is invigorating. You sense amazement and jealousy from people in the crowd. You hear your bandmate cheering you on and exclaiming her pride from across the hall. As the song ends, everyone returns to their dining and socializing. You walk away from the drums and sit with the other musicians in the chairs that line the stage. You are speechless that you just played with arguably, the greatest band, in rock and roll history. You will never forget October 9th, 2011. And now, it is just another memory.

Thank You

. . . .

The greatest expense in life is time. Once it is given, it is forever spent. Thank you beyond measure for giving me the gift of your time. Multitudinous appreciation and countless blessings!

- Kristen

Quote from Freud

. . . .

"I may say at once that I am no connoisseur in art, but simply a layman. I have often observed that the subject matter of works of art has a stronger attraction for me than their formal and technical qualities, though to the artist their value lies first and foremost in these latter. I am unable rightly to appreciate many of the methods used and the effects obtained in art.... Nevertheless, works of art do exercise a powerful effect on me, especially those of literature and sculpture, less often of painting. This has occasioned me, when I have been contemplating such things, to spend a long time before them trying to apprehend them in my own way, i.e., to explain to myself what their effect is due to. Wherever I cannot do this, as for instance with music, I am almost incapable of obtaining any pleasure. Some rationalistic, or perhaps analytic, turn of mind in me rebels against being moved by a thing without knowing why I am thus affected and what it is that affects me".

— Sigmund Freud, *"The Moses of Michelangelo"* (1914), Standard Edition, Vol. XIII, p. 211.